M000310508

the art of
Calm
Living

how to find peace
in your life

An Hachette UK Company
www.hachette.co.uk

First published in Great Britain in 2022 by Pyramid,
an imprint of Octopus Publishing Group Ltd.
Carmelite House
50 Victoria Embankment
London, EC4Y 0DZ
www.octopusbooks.co.uk

Distributed in the US by
Hachette Book Group
1290 Avenue of the Americas
4th and 5th Floors
New York, NY 10104

Distributed in Canada by
Canadian Manda Group
664 Annette St.
Toronto, Ontario, Canada M6S 2C8

ISBN: 978-0-7537-3493-3

A CIP catalogue record for this book is available from the British Library

Printed and bound in China

10 9 8 7 6 5 4 3 2

Publisher: Lucy Pessell
Designer: Hannah Coughlin
Junior Editor: Sarah Kennedy
Editorial Assistant: Emily Martin
Production Controller: Lisa Pinnell

the art of
Calm
Living

how to find peace
in your life

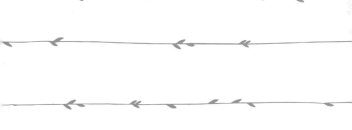

introduction

In our modern-day world, it is easy to become bogged down in the everyday. We have become so busy – whether it's with work, keeping our home in order, caring for our family, seeing our friends – that we're often left rushing from one place to the next without a second thought for ourselves. When things go wrong, we tend to put up with them, passing off our worries as simply "just a part of life", ignoring the fact that these events can leave us overwhelmed, burned out and even with feelings of anxiety and depression. But it doesn't have to be this way.

The frenetic pace of modern life may not be conducive to cultivating a calm mindset, yet it is precisely this inner calm that will equip us to deal with our life, no matter what challenges it presents. Each of us has the power to connect to our true selves, to retreat into silence and find serenity in even the stormiest of times. Our circumstances are often beyond our control, but our reaction to them is very much within our grasp. We can choose calm in the most stressful of situations. We can find stillness in among the chaos.

The Art of Calm Living brings you ideas on how to cultivate calm daily, through acceptance, a change of pace, releasing tension, finding perspective and spiralling inward to a place of tranquility. You'll find exercises, tips and inspirational quotes to help you breeze through the daily grind with grace and ease.

Don't let any more time slip through your fingers in a haze of rushing, worrying, striving and stressing. Use this book as your guide, inspiration and motivation to let go of those emotions that no longer serve you, to slow down, simplify, appreciate and to find a place of peace within – one day at a time – until calm becomes a way of life.

how to use this book

This handy little book is small enough that you can easily keep it nearby – perhaps on your bedside table or in your bag – ready for whenever you need a moment of calmness. Work your way through it from cover to cover or dip into it whenever you like; bookmark your favourite pages or make a note of tips that you want to get better at practising.

You may find that some of the tips in the book work better for you than others. That's completely fine, and is all part of your journey to living a life that truly brings you peace and calmness. You may find that you need to practise some of the exercises and tips before you can truly master them and apply them to your life. Learning to be calm in stressful situations – especially the ones that really test us – doesn't happen overnight. It takes patience and lots of practise, so don't be frustrated if these tips don't work for you straight away. Keep at it, and you are sure to find what works for you.

accept your feelings

Calmness is a huge gift. And once you master it, you will
be able to respond in a useful way to every difficult situation
that decides to walk into your heart.

Geri Larkin, founder and former headteacher of Still Point
Zen Buddhist Temple

When negative feelings creep into our hearts and minds,
it's natural to want to try and bury them deep down in the
hope that they'll go away so we won't have to face them.
But this is going to do far more harm than good.

If something is causing you distress or making you angry, it
is disrupting your inner calm, so don't avoid the emotion.
Try to get in touch with the feelings, not in a confrontational
way but rather just to acknowledge and accept them. Note
that the emotion is transient and will pass.

retain perspective

Expectation feeds frustration. It is an unhealthy attachment to people, things, and outcomes we wish we could control, but don't.

Dr Steve Maraboli, speaker, author and behavioural scientist

With the pressures and busyness of everyday life, it's so easy to fall into a tunnel-vision way of living, focusing on the smaller picture and obsessing over the tiniest flaws and mistakes we make. However, those small mistakes make us human, and, in the end, they really don't matter.

So don't add unnecessary stress to everyday ordeals, most of which are trivial. Unless it's a life-or-death situation, remind yourself that it really doesn't matter that much. Retaining perspective in this way will allow you to live a much calmer, happier and more fulfilled life.

commit to yoga

Yoga practice helps me stay present and focus on the now,
which is kryptonite to my inner saboteur.

RuPaul, drag queen, actor, model and television personality

Immersing yourself fully is the best way to reap the benefits
of this wonderful, calming and life-enhancing practice.
However, if your everyday life is particularly busy and
you often find yourself struggling to find time in the day,
having to commit to a yoga class can sometimes feel like a
bit of a chore.

So instead of signing up to weekly classes, commit to
practising yoga at home for 30 days in a row. There are lots
of free online resources and also several videos to choose
from on YouTube. Just 20 minutes a day will go a long way
toward honing your skill, making yoga a habit and a way
of life. But if you find yourself pushed for time, even just a
few minutes will make a difference. Don't fall into the trap
of "all or nothing", and do what you can, when you can.

wind down with some mellow music

Music and rhythm find their way into the secret places of the soul.

Plato, philosopher

Listening to gentle music is a great way to finish off your day and help you feel more clam. Research suggests that your brain waves will sync up with the slow rhythm of the soothing music, putting you in a meditative state.

Make a playlist of songs and music that relax you, and have it ready to go on your phone whenever you're in need of some soothing. If you're having trouble nodding off at night, you can also set a timer on your phone and try falling asleep to the music.

don't take on too much in the day

Slow down and enjoy life. It's not only the scenery you miss by
going too fast – you also miss the sense of where you are going
and why.

Eddie Cantor, performer, comedian, dancer, singer and songwriter

When we're busy and our to-do lists feel about a mile long,
it can be tempting to squeeze lots of tasks and events into
one day in an attempt to free up the next one. However, if
you try and cram too much into your day, you're only going
to end up feeling overwhelmed, exhausted and burned out.

Every now and then, put aside a day to concentrate on
yourself and do things at your own pace. Don't be afraid
to cancel plans if necessary. You'll find you become better
at listening to your body and mind, and, over time, will be
able to plan your day much more effectively.

be grateful

Calmness is the lake of mind, thankfulness is the lake of heart.

Unknown

When we practise gratitude, our bodies produce feel-good chemicals, boosting our mood and helping us to feel calmer. Many studies have shown that gratitude can make a huge difference in our lives.

Practise gratitude as a way to calmly accept your life as it is right now. Engage in the daily habit of listing all the things you are grateful for instead of focusing on what you want and don't have. Do this by making a list of 3–5 things from your day that you are grateful for and recording them on your phone or a notepad by your bed – somewhere easy to access and remember so you don't forget. After a few days of doing this, you will start to notice the added calm this brings to your life.

let go

Sometimes letting things go is an act of far greater power than
defending or hanging on.

Eckhart Tolle, author and spiritual teacher

Letting go can be hard, but sometimes it's the only option.
This can mean a number of things, such as letting go of
toxic relationships in your life, or a job that leaves you
feeling stressed and undervalued, or even letting go of
material possessions that aren't serving you as well as
they once did.

While not easy, letting go of things ultimately relieves
a huge amount of pain and pressure in our minds and
hearts, and, in the long run, will help you to lead a much
calmer life. Letting go of something could even open a
door and lead to an exciting new opportunity. Trust your
instincts, be brave and let go.

limit distractions

A distracted existence leads us to no goal.

Johann Wolfgang von Goethe, playwright, novelist and scientist

When we're trying to focus on ourselves in order to reach a calmer state of mind, there are lots of distractions that can interrupt us – technology being the biggest culprit.

Try to spend some time away from your devices every day. Shut down your computer and leave your phone in another room, even if it's just for an hour or two. Constantly filling your mind with the news or social media isn't going to do you any favours when trying to reach a calmer state of mind.

If you find this hard to do, start by giving up your devices for half an hour or so, and gradually increase it to an hour, a few hours, and so on. The more you do it, the more you'll realize you really don't need your phone on you all the time in order to function.

find work you enjoy

If you're happy in what you're doing, you'll like yourself,
you'll have inner peace. And if you have that, along with
physical health, you'll have more success than you could
possibly have imagined.

*Roger Caras, wildlife photographer and preservationist, author and
television personality*

If you are in a job you don't enjoy – and many of us are –
do everything you can to find another. Explore what's out
there and how you could become involved in things that
truly speak to you. If you can find work that you love, you
will be far more at peace with yourself.

Bear in mind, however, that this doesn't mean having to
find a dream job or a job that sounds flashy and exciting.
It could be a fairly "ordinary-sounding" job, but if it
involves tasks that you know will leave you feeling satisfied
and fulfilled rather than stressed out and constantly
pressurized, you'll find yourself on the path to a much
calmer life.

practise nadi shodhana

Breath is the power behind all things... I breathe in and know that good things will happen.

Tao Porchon-Lynch, yoga master and writer

Practise the powerful technique of Nadi Shodhana, or alternate nostril breathing, to soothe an anxious mind:

1. Sit up tall in sukhasana (cross-legged). Relax your left hand on your lap and bring your right hand to your face.

2. Close your right nostril with your right thumb and inhale through the left nostril slowly and steadily. Pause at the top and retain your breath for a count of two.

3. Switch sides so your index finger now seals the left nostril and exhale slowly through your right nostril.

4. Pause briefly at the bottom and then inhale deeply through the right nostril. Pause at the top and retain your breath for a count of two.

5. Switch sides so your thumb now seals the right nostril and exhale slowly through your left nostril. Repeat the cycle above 5–10 times.

go for a gentle swim

If there is magic on this planet, it is contained in water.

Loren Eiseley, anthropologist, philosopher and natural science writer

Swimming is a particularly good way to relax the body and soothe the mind. Instead of powering on through the water, consider swimming slowly as a more restorative practice, letting the water hold and soothe you.

If you're feeling very tense and wound up, you might want to give wild swimming a try. It may not sound especially calming, but the cold water will help to release excess adrenaline from your body, working to relieve any pent-up tension that can otherwise be tricky to get rid of.

18

get organized

Gentleness is strength under control. It is the ability to stay
calm, no matter what happens.

Elizabeth George, writer

Many stressful situations are avoidable if you prepare
ahead of time, whether it's tasks at work, chores around the
house or travelling to see friends and family.

If you're ever in doubt about a certain situation, make a
list of everything that needs doing beforehand. Note down
things like deadlines, items you may need, directions (if
you're travelling somewhere) and anything else you might
need to remember.

Getting things down on to paper will relieve the pressure
of having a hundred different things rushing around in
your head at the same time, and will help you feel more in
control of the situation, whatever it may be.

be kind to yourself

You are worthy of every drop of sweetness and ease that you encounter.

Alex Elle, writer

When you're having a bad day, it's important to show yourself some kindness and to not beat yourself up over the things bothering you.

Put aside some time in the evening just for yourself. Go for a walk, take a bath, cook yourself a great meal, treat yourself to your favourite dessert – do whatever makes you feel happy and calm.

Rest assured that whatever's bothering you today, tomorrow is a completely new chance to try again.

connect with nature

Look at a tree, a flower, a plant. Let your awareness rest upon it. How still they are, how deeply rooted in Being. Allow nature to teach you stillness.

Eckhart Tolle, spiritual teacher and author

Find a quiet place free from the mental noise that fills our everyday lives. Even in the city, you can look up at the sky, find a green space, feel the wind on your face…

If you live near to a wooded area, practice the Japanese art of shinrin-yoku – "forest bathing". This is exactly what it sounds like – spend some time sitting amongst the trees and listening to the sound of nature around you. What can you see, hear and smell? The health benefits of this are so effective that doctors now recommend shinrin-yoku to their patients for increased happiness and wellbeing.

leave the past behind

Let go of the battle. Breathe quietly and let it be.

Jack Kornfield, author

So many of the stresses and worries that ruin our sense of calm are rooted firmly in the past. Stop indulging in negative ruminations over events that have already happened and concentrate on today.

If you find that past mistakes and negative experiences keep popping into your head, try to view them in a different light. What did you learn from these past experiences? How have they changed the way you do things for the better?

Turn each bad memory on its head and it'll soon lose its ability to keep you down.

massage your hands

The hand is the visible part of the brain.

Immanuel Kant, philosopher

For a quick massage on the go, try massaging your hands.
We hold a lot of our tension here so releasing this is a
simple route to feeling more relaxed. A hand massage
is especially good to do before bedtime, and, while not
necessary, lotions and oils can help to heighten the
experience. You may also find it helps to warm your hands
up a bit before you start.

Massage one hand at a time, using as much pressure as is
comfortable for you. A good massage should last about five
minutes per hand, and don't forget to massage your fingers all
the way down to their tips, as well as the back of your hand.

recite calming mantras

The words you speak become the house you live in.

Hafiz, poet

Write some calming mantras that you can call upon in times of stress. For example, "I can handle this situation calmly and with good grace." Close your eyes and repeat the mantra to yourself whenever needed.

It may feel strange to do at first, but the more you practise reciting mantras to yourself, the calmer you will start to feel. This is because you are what you think, and your thoughts create your own reality because your brain will believe what it's being told, even if, in the moment, you feel anxious and stressed.

find your calm place

Within you there is a stillness and a sanctuary to which you
can retreat at any time and be yourself.

Hermann Hesse, poet, novelist and painter

You don't have to travel anywhere to do this, simply bring
to mind a place – either real or imagined – that engenders
feelings of peace. Consider drawing or writing about your
"calm place" in order to make it more real and therefore
reachable in times of turmoil.

What can you see, hear, smell or taste? Why do these
things help you to feel calm? Can you recreate them in
your everyday life? For example, if, in your calm place you
can hear the sound of rain on the window, search for rain
sounds online and listen to them whenever you're in need
of some calm in your life.

don't put pressure on yourself

Excellence is not being the best, it's doing your best.

Unknown

Nowadays, it's harder than ever to escape the pressures of having to be "successful". Our social media feeds are flooded with images of people going on expensive holidays, buying houses, getting high-paying jobs, getting married... the list goes on. When you're seeing these images every day – often first thing in the morning and last thing at night, as many of us are guilty of doing – you start to believe that everyone is more successful than you and that you are underachieving.

This is, of course, not true. The images you see on social media are just a tiny portion of people's lives, while the hardships that we all go through never make it to the internet. You don't need to be the best at everything – earning a high salary, getting straight As, being the best friend, the best mother, first over the line at everything. Find true inner calm by accepting yourself wherever you're at today.

get creative

Creativity is intelligence having fun.

Albert Einstein, theoretical physicist

There is a proven relationship between getting hands-on creative – whether cooking, painting, knitting, sketching, sculpting or sewing – and relaxation. Studies have shown that indulging in such creative hobbies lowers the heart rate and blood pressure, actively calming the nervous system.

There are lots of ways you can become more creative. Many communities have knitting and sewing clubs, so head to your local library and see if they have any information on what's available. You can also join classes led by professionals, or, if you'd rather get creative from the comfort of your own home, there are plenty of videos and posts online – whether it's Instagram, YouTube or Pinterest.

make time for
your friends

**A true friend is one who overlooks your broken fence and
admires the flowers in your garden.**

Unknown

Spending time with loved ones increases our levels of the
feel-good hormone oxytocin, plus there's nothing more
calming than talking worries through with good friends.
Arrange to meet for a drink after work, get some retail
therapy in, watch a movie together – whatever you and
your loved ones like to do.

If you often find that you forget to make time for your
loved ones because of how busy you are in the day, make
sure to schedule times into your calendar days, weeks (or
even months!) in advance that are reserved just for you
and your friends. And make sure to stick to those dates and
plan work around them. Remember, work should revolve
around the rest of your life – not the other way around.

prep for bed

Sometimes the most urgent and vital thing you can possibly
do is take a complete rest.

Ashleigh Brilliant, author

Lack of sleep has all kinds of negative impacts of our
health and wellbeing. It's pretty impossible to find inner
peace and remain calm in difficult situations when you're
feeling frazzled, so put some effort into getting a good
night's sleep.

Make your bedroom a comfortable, calm haven with
plenty of clear space. Try and stick to the same calming
bedtime routine every night – simple rituals such as having
a bath or reading a book can become signifiers to your
brain to relax.

Also try and make sure that your room is at a cool enough
temperature for you to sleep comfortably, and that no
excess light is getting in.

practise compassion

We can't heal the world today, but we can begin with a voice of compassion, a heart of love, an act of kindness.

Mary Davis, social entrepreneur, activist and campaigner

Inner peace is difficult to attain if you are constantly focused on yourself and your own worries. When you make the time to care for others and practise compassion, you become a more positive, peaceful person. It can be something as small as complimenting someone on their clothing, helping an elderly person to cross the road or volunteering for your favourite charity.

Showing kindness to others is also contagious. When you brighten one person's day, they are more likely to do the same for someone else, continuing the chain reaction of compassion and kindness.

seek out the bright side

You must keep looking on the bright side, because you won't find anything in the dark.

Zack W. Van, writer

Practise optimism wherever possible. Turn negatives into positives and find a reason to smile – there is always at least one!

As you may have already read earlier on in this book, you are what you think. The more you fill your mind with positive and happy thoughts – even if you really don't feel in the mood to – the calmer you will start to feel on the bad days. It may feel strange at first, but just give it a try and you'll be amazed at the results.

You can also try practising gratitude and using a notebook to write down the good parts of your day (see page 13).

be early

Better three hours too soon than a minute too late.

William Shakespeare, playwright

Plan to arrive everywhere ten minutes early and say goodbye to frantic rushing and sweat-inducing commutes. You'll find this makes getting to work and social events a lot less anxiety-creating, especially if you find travelling on busy public transport overwhelming.

The next time you're on the train or bus or in your car, relax and listen to your favourite music, podcast or audiobook, safe in the knowledge that you have plenty of time in case of any unexpected delays.

play with a pet

The ideal of calm exists in a sitting cat.

Jules Renard, writer

There are many benefits of playing with your dog or cat, and studies have shown that interacting with animals can ease tension and promote peace of mind.

Additionally, playing with your pet is more likely to get you moving and active and can therefore help to boost your mood. Interacting with your dog or cat can also help to tackle feelings of isolation and loneliness.

If you don't have a pet, offer to look after a friend's or family member's the next time they go on holiday. Or, if you'd like to commit to owning your own cat or dog, there are plenty of shelters and rescue centres from which you can adopt your own furry friend.

33

worry less

Happy is the person who can keep a quiet heart, in the chaos and tumult of this modern world.

Patience Strong, poet

Worrying won't change the outcome of any event, but it will take away your peace of mind today. Each time you find yourself worrying about something, try to replace that worry with a positive thought about that person or event.

It is, of course, easier said than done to simply worry less, but the more you tell yourself the above – that worrying about something isn't going to change the outcome – the calmer you will start to feel. Practise makes perfect, so the more you do it, the more instinctive it will become.

practise patience

One minute of patience, ten years of peace.

Greek proverb

There are many advantages to practising patience in your everyday life. You'll experience better mental health, as exercising patience can help us keep our thoughts in control. You will become better at reaching important decisions, and you will also find you have more time for the most treasured things in your life, like your family and friends.

Practise being patient whenever you can. You can do this every day in many small ways – don't automatically opt for the shortest queue in the supermarket or the traffic-free route with no hold-ups. Instead, choose to put yourself in these more frustrating situations, and choose to stay calm.

step outside

Look at a tree, how calm, lovely and beautiful she is. She is
always meditating for the love of the sun.

Dr Debasish Mridha, physician, philosopher and author

If you spend much of your working day indoors, make
an effort to step outside on your lunch break. Leave your
to-do list behind and let the fresh air clear your head. If
possible, walk to a green space such as a park or public
garden and let the soothing qualities of your surrounds
wash over you. Taking a break every day, no matter how
short, can do wonders for your overall happiness and
mental health, and will help you to lead a calmer life.

Getting outside for a walk is also a great way of getting
your blood pumping and raising your heart rate. It is
recommended that you get at least 150 minutes of walking
every week, which is roughly a 20-minute walk every day.

make use of lavender

Mother nature has the power to please, to comfort, to calm,
and to nurture one's soul.

Anthony Douglas Williams, spiritualist, writer and animal activist

Nothing beats all the different smells that mother nature
has to offer us – from the scent of the rain to the fragrance
of blooming flowers in the spring and summer. But for
the days when you're feeling overwhelmed, there are
certain aromas that can help to restore your sense of calm,
such as lavender.

There are lots of ways to incorporate the smell of lavender
into your home, such as lavender-scented candles, putting
lavender oil into a diffuser or simply keeping bunches of
it in pretty vases around the house. You can also buy a
lavender pillow spray to spray onto your pillow and duvet
before going to sleep. This will help to soothe any late-
night worries and will let you doze off that bit faster.

notice your reaction

Life is 10% what happens to you, and 90% how you react to it.

Charles R. Swindoll, pastor and author

Focus on your senses when you're feeling wound up or stressed. Notice how your palms are sweaty or your heart is beating faster. Don't judge these reactions, just calmly acknowledge them and your body will switch out of its automatic stress response far more quickly.

Knowing the physical signs of stress and anxiety is also useful for anticipating when you might need to take a break. For example, if, when you are stressed, you know you tend to breathe faster, take this as your cue to stop what you are doing and a have a few minutes' breather.

breathe

Take a deep breath. Inhale peace. Exhale happiness.

A.D. Posey, writer

When you're feeling stressed, breathe. Use the breath as the powerful tool it is in countering the body's natural response to stress by taking the following steps:

1. Close your eyes, place your hands on your lower ribcage and take a deep breath in. Feel your breath travelling downward and the expansion of your belly against your hands as you inhale deeply.

2. Exhale slowly and fully until all the air has exited your lungs, imagining all the stress leaving your body as you do so.

3. Repeat steps 1 and 2 five times.

39

prioritize

Set peace of mind as your highest goal, and organize your life around it.

Brian Tracy, motivational speaker and author

So you have hundreds of things to do, and no time to do them all. Step back and prioritize. What really needs to be done today and what can wait until tomorrow? You'll be surprised at how much of your to-do list falls into the latter category and just how much "stuff" you're unnecessarily fretting about.

You can even go one step further than this – what can you drop completely from your to-do list? What are the things that simply don't matter? Are these things that you're doing for yourself or feel pressured to do by others? In times of stress, the best thing to do in order to reach a state of calm is to prioritize yourself.

have a pyjama day

Take rest. A field that has rested gives a bountiful crop.

Ovid, poet

When your life is filled with busyness – whether it's work, seeing friends, caring for your family or keeping your home in order – it can be hard to put aside time to concentrate on yourself.

Take a day to completely withdraw and wind down. Stay in your pyjamas, snuggle up on the couch and shut out the hustle of the outside world. Watch a movie, read a book, do whatever makes you feel calm and relaxed, and enjoy the cosy haven of your home for the whole day.

When you take the time to completely switch off, you're giving your brain a chance to recover and have a proper break. If you do this regularly, you will notice you become much better at dealing with stressful situations and will be able to reach a state of calm much more quickly.

make a big task small

It's the steady, quiet, plodding ones who win in the lifelong race.

Robert W. Service, poet and writer

Sometimes when we look at our to-do lists, it can be hard to know where to even start – especially if we're feeling particularly under pressure from important tasks and looming deadlines.

If it's a seemingly insurmountable task that's disrupting your inner calm, break it down into smaller manageable tasks, which will instantly make it feel more achievable. Take one small step at a time and you'll soon find yourself at the top of the mountain. And if you're finding it hard to get going even on the little tasks, remember that all you need to do is simply start and the rest will follow. Sometimes you need to get it wrong to get it right, so don't be afraid to dive straight in and get started on things.

be flexible

You find peace by coming to terms with what you don't know.

Nassim Nicholas Taleb, essayist and statistician

No matter how carefully we plan, things will always crop up unexpectedly. Always prepare to be flexible and adapt to changing situations so your body's stress responses are not automatically triggered when things don't go exactly as you'd hoped.

If you're the kind of person who likes to have everything planned to a T, who likes to stick to their list of to-dos without deviating from it, try and go for one day without doing this. Rather than religiously sticking to a routine, just do things as they come up or as and when you feel ready to do them. This will show you that you don't always have to be in complete control of everything in order to feel calm.

seek support

Don't be afraid to ask questions. Don't be afraid to ask for help when you need it. I do that every day. Asking for help isn't a sign of weakness: it's a sign of strength. It shows you have the courage to admit when you don't know something, and to learn something new.

Barack Obama, 44th US president

Don't carry the world on your shoulders and try to do everything yourself. At work, delegate and seek support from colleagues to avoid an unnecessary build-up of stress. Engage in teamwork to relieve the anxiety of feeling like you have sole responsibility for everything.

The same goes for when you're at home. If you find things like the washing up or laundry keep piling up, share out the duties between you and your partner or your housemates. You could even make a rota of duties to put up on the fridge so that everyone can make sure they are lending a hand.

tell the truth

Speaking your truth is the most powerful tool we all have.

Oprah Winfrey, talk show host

Being open and honest leads to a calm state of mind. If you have nothing to hide you will be more at peace with yourself. Whereas if you find yourself telling lies – even just the odd white lie – to try and cover things up, you will find you become exhausted by having to keep track of everything you've said for fear of being found out. And while telling a lie may help you feel "safe", there is no long-term happiness to be found in not speaking your truth.

So while it may not be easy, the next time you find yourself tempted to lie about something, push past the fear and tell the truth instead.

45

know your stress triggers

Anger is an acid that can do more harm to the vessel in which it is stored than anything on which it is poured.

Mark Twain, writer

Look at how you react to tricky situations and ask yourself the reasons why. Understanding what really pushes your buttons and winds you up into a stressed state of mind is the first step in letting it go.

Once you've identified the situations that get you worked up, ask yourself – can these situations be avoided? Are you able to remove yourself either by stepping outside for some fresh air or by taking a few deep breaths and rising above it? It's easier said than done, but it's important that you are in control of your emotions, rather than the other way around.

choose calm

The chaos doesn't end. You kinda just become the calm.

Nikki Rowe, writer

You alone are responsible for your own reactions to any situation. You can choose your behaviour at any given moment. Mentally prepare yourself for difficult situations and envisage your calm and measured response.

It may be the case that you have to go through a few stressful situations before you work out how you best respond to stress, and you may have to make a few mistakes before you get it right. But once you think you've worked out the best approach, make a note of it and practise it again and again until you've mastered it. It may be a little painful along the way, but do your best and the benefits will be worth it.

clear the clutter

Travel light, live light, spread the light, be the light.

Yogi Bhajan, entrepreneur, yoga teacher and spiritual teacher

Your home should be your haven, a place where you can escape from the pressures of everyday life. Studies have shown it's much harder to do this when you're surrounded by clutter. So today, set some time aside to clear out those items you no longer want or need and create a calm space you can truly relax in.

Sometimes tidying up and decluttering can seem like a mammoth task, so if you aren't sure where to start, begin with one room and move on to the others whenever you next have some free time. You might find it beneficial to start with your bedroom first, as this is where you're most likely to need a sense of peace and calm. Make sure you begin early enough in the day so that you are able to leave time for breaks so you don't get fed up halfway through.

use pmr

To relax is not to collapse, but simply to undo tension.

Vanda Scaravelli, yoga teacher

Use progressive muscle relaxation (PMR) techniques. This involves lying down with your eyes closed and moving through all the muscle groups in your body, clenching them tight for five seconds, then releasing.

PMR is especially good for reducing feelings of anxiety, tension and stress. It can also improve the quality of your sleep, as well as counter problems such as neck pain and back pain – both of which are all too common among office workers who are hunched over a laptop or computer all day. Try PMR once a day for a week or so to truly start to feel its calming effects.

49

drink yogi tea

There is no trouble so great or grave that cannot be
diminished by a nice cup of tea.

Bernard-Paul Heroux, philosopher

Soothe your soul with a cup of calming yogi tea. Boil up
together:

1 cup water

2–3 slices of fresh root ginger

½ cinnamon stick

3–4 cloves

3–4 black peppercorns

5–7 green cardamom pods

Black tea leaves, to taste

Milk, to taste

Honey, to taste (optional)

wrap yourself in love

Surround yourself only with people who are going to lift you higher.

Oprah Winfrey, talk show host

We've all been in a situation where we've been spending time with a "friend" only to leave feeling exhausted and worn out. Perhaps they've spent the entire time talking about themselves or maybe they've been glancing at their phone one too many times, not listening to what you have to say.

Surround yourself with people you love and who love you to achieve inner serenity. Life is far too short to be spending time with anyone who makes you feel small or inadequate in any way.

51

lose the adrenaline

The hurrier I go, the behinder I get.

Lewis Carroll, novelist

Try to avoid leading an adrenaline-fuelled lifestyle, which will impact your health and your peace of mind. Slow down and you'll be both healthier and happier.

If, at the end of a busy day, you feel like your body is filled with excess adrenaline, go for a run or a walk to help burn some of it off. It's important that you do this before trying to relax or wind down for bed, as any surplus energy or adrenaline is only going to leave you feeling restless and agitated. You'll find yourself in a constant loop of trying to relax only to become annoyed at the fact that you aren't able to, which, in turn, will lead to you becoming even more tense.

meditate

Meditation is not a way of making your mind quiet. It is a way
of entering into the quiet that is already there – buried under
the 50,000 thoughts the average person thinks every day.

Deepak Chopra, author

Find your inner silence through meditation. You don't
have to have practised meditation before – there are many
guided meditation apps or YouTube videos available for
everyone. Meditate for as long as you like, or according to
however much time you have spare in the day. Don't fall
into the trap of the "all or nothing" mindset; even just a
few short moments a day can make a difference to your
overall wellbeing.

Meditation is especially good for creating a sense of calm
at the end of a long day. It can help you to gain perspective
and clarity in particularly stressful situations, helping to
reduce negative thoughts and feelings of anxiety.

choose your
words carefully

**If there were a little more silence, if we all kept quiet…maybe
we could understand something.**

Federico Fellini, film director

How often do you truly stop to listen to someone during a
conversation? How often are you thinking, instead, about
what you're going to say next? Can you honestly say that you
take the time to reflect upon what a person has said before
you reply? And how often have you said something without
thinking it through first, only for it to end up "coming out
the wrong way" and hurting somebody's feelings?

Don't let your inner chatter spill out – say nothing unless
it's true, kind or useful. And don't rush to say something
just to fill the silence – really think about the impact
your words are having on the person you are talking to.
It doesn't matter if you can't think of anything to say;
sometimes it's enough just to listen.

walk

As you start to walk on the way, the way appears.

Rumi, poet

Take a five-minute walk outside, and leave all electronic devices at home or on your desk. Simply listen to your footsteps and observe your surroundings. You will return with a quieter mind.

Walking is a great way to start your day, and it can be especially peaceful to head out early in the morning when there aren't many people around. Starting your day off with a slow, peaceful walk is an ideal chance to set your intention for the day and to think about what you want to achieve. Or, you can pick up the pace a bit and go for a brisk walk or steady jog to get your blood flowing and your brain clear of fog, ready to start the day with a sense of ease and clarity.

accept yourself

Without judgment, we let each thing, event, day, and feeling be whatever it is.

Melody Beattie, author

Reframe what you regard as your negative characteristics into positive ones to help you along the path toward self-acceptance. You will only ever find inner peace if you truly accept yourself for who you are, and you will only ever truly love others once you have learned to love yourself.

Think of some uplifting messages about what you like about yourself – whether it's a personality trait or a certain part of your body – and write them on some sticky notes. Then, stick them up on your mirror or wardrobe door so that you see them every morning and are reminded of all the incredible things that make you you. You'll find that by doing this, all those "flaws" you thought you had are just part of what makes you unique.

live in the moment

Yesterday is ashes, tomorrow wood. Only today does the fire burn brightly.

Inuit proverb

Being completely present in the moment will enhance feelings of calm and contentment. Practise a mindfulness meditation to ground yourself in the now. Or simply look out of the window and observe the colour of the sky, take a sip of your coffee and notice the sensation as it glides down your throat, feel the warmth of the mug, the feel of your clothes against your skin, the light from the window in the room…

By living in the moment, you will become aware of all the wonderful things in life to be grateful for, no matter how small, and will be able to live with a greater sense of clarity and purpose.

release stress

Relaxation comes from letting go of tense thoughts.

Frances Wilshire, writer

When stress becomes a "natural" part of your day, it's easy to stop noticing the effects it's having on your mind and body. You can grow accustomed to dealing with it, thinking you have it all in hand. But the longer you stay in a state of stress, the more likely you are to slip into the danger zone of becoming burned out, overworked and exhausted. It's therefore extremely important to make sure you have an outlet during stressful times in order to ease the strain of carrying all that pressure on your shoulders.

Curse into your pillow, cry if you want to, phone a friend, doodle your way to distraction, go for a run, organize a fun night out. Whatever you do, don't keep stressful feelings locked inside – they'll only grow into something too big to handle, which is a much harder issue to solve.

indulge in "me time"

Loving yourself isn't vanity. It's sanity.

André Gide, author

Taking time out for yourself away from the constant demands of your life is essential if you are to achieve a balanced state of mind.

Do whatever makes you happy, and spend some time focusing on nobody else but yourself – whether it's taking yourself out for a dinner and theatre trip, treating yourself to a weekend away or simply taking a long bath and spending the evening buried under the duvet watching a favourite movie.

Looking after yourself is just as important as looking after your family and friends – you can only do a good job at the latter if you take care of the former. So don't feel guilty about doing something for yourself.

be positive

When the odds are hopeless, when all seems to be lost, then is the time to be calm.

Ian Fleming, author

Maintain a positive outlook and your path to inner peace will be a far less rocky one. The more we are able to look on the bright side, the better we are able to deal calmly with stressful situations that are beyond our control.

The best way to start seeing things in a positive light is to start practising gratitude. Follow the advice on page 13 about keeping a note of all the things in your life to be grateful for.

Adopting a more positive outlook in our lives can increase self-esteem and boost our overall mood and wellbeing. It's not about ignoring your current problems – it's about seeing them in different ways in order to overcome them.

from mind to body

If you get the inside right, the outside will fall into place.

Eckhart Tolle, author and spiritual teacher

To achieve calm in moments of stress, switch your focus from your mind to your body. Instead of replaying a frustrating situation over and over in your head, focus instead on your body using the below exercise:

1. Find a quiet place to sit and simply notice the feel of the chair beneath you.

2. Sit up tall and relax your shoulders, and try to bring your shoulder blades together.

3. Inhale through your nose for a count of four, hold for two and exhale through your mouth for seven.

4. Repeat this cycle at least five times.

This will calm your chattering mind, just as the depth of breath will calm your nervous system.

practise tai chi

Everything we do is infused with the energy with which
we do it. If we're frantic, life will be frantic. If we're peaceful,
life will be peaceful.

*Marianne Williamson, author, spiritual leader
and political activist*

Tai Chi is an ancient Chinese tradition, and nowadays is
practised as a gentle and graceful form of exercise. It is low
impact so can be practised by anyone, no matter your level
of fitness. It can also be practised wherever you like – in
your living room or out in a green, open space like your
local park. If you're not sure where to start, see if there are
any classes in your area. If not, there are plenty of online
resources to make the most of.

Tai Chi's focus on deep breathing, meditation and gentle
flowing movements is a wonderful calming tool. It can be
used to lessen feelings of stress and anxiety and is also a great
way to gently move your body and stretch your muscles.

pay attention to
what you eat

In my food world there is no fear or guilt, only joy
and balance.

Ellie Krieger, dietitian and nutritionist

In times of stress it's natural to want to reach for cake or
other sugary treats for instant comfort. However, the sharp
spike in your blood sugar levels is only going to make
you feel more jittery. Making healthier snack choices can
actually reduce stress – research suggests, for example, that
the vitamin C in fruits decreases stress-induced free radicals.

Also try making your meals from scratch using nutritional
whole foods and enjoy the meditative process that cooking
can be. Cooking a delicious meal can be a means of
winding down at the end of a long day.

bring the outside in

Adopt the pace of nature: her secret is patience.

Ralph Waldo Emerson, philosopher and abolitionist

Potted plants and flowers bring nature into your home, and will also help to create a cosy, inviting atmosphere. Having flowers and plants nearby will calm an anxious mind.

Plants like snake plant and aloe vera are great for purifying the air in your home, and plants such as jasmine and lavender will aid relaxation. The last two are more commonly grown outdoors, but can easily be brought inside too – just look up advice online on how to best look after them.

write it down

Write down the thoughts of the moment. Those that come unsought for are commonly the most valuable.

Francis Bacon, philosopher

Get whatever is bothering you down on paper. This cathartic process of writing about your frustrations will really help to clear your mind.

You also probably find that any problems that seem like monumental hurdles in your mind actually lose some of their power and hold over you. As you write them down, you will gain perspective on them and will be able to see them in a different light.

Writing things down is also useful if you can't quite pinpoint what is bothering you. Just write down whatever comes into your head and go from there. This will help you to trace your negative feelings back to their roots and will enable you to tackle them more head on.

hug a tree

Step outside for a while – calm your mind. It is better to hug a tree than to bang your head against a wall continually.

Rasheed Ogunlaru, life, business and corporate coach

Many tree species are believed to have a specific calming effect on both the mind and body. Pick a tree that appeals to you and hug it for a few moments, absorbing its calming energy. If you feel a bit too self-conscious doing this, just sit against the tree's trunk for a little while.

Trees are considered to represent wisdom, power and prosperity. It can be incredibly humbling to know that the tree you have just hugged or are sitting against could be hundreds of years old, having survived harsh winter storms or searing heat in the summertime. Think about all the children who may have climbed the tree, how many people the tree has offered shade or shelter to. Think about how vast its root system is, deep underground. How can you apply this feeling of being rooted to your own life?

streamline your diary

To find peace, sometimes you have to be willing to lose your connection with the people, places and things that create all the noise in your life.

Unknown

Cut out all unnecessary obligations and learn how to say no. It can be hard to do at first, but learning to say no to the things that you don't want to do will put you in control of your life and will leave you feeling calmer at the end of your day.

If you aren't entirely sure how to say no without coming across as rude, here are some simple ways to put your foot down:

"Let me think about that first and get back to you."

"I'm afraid I can't commit to this, as I have other priorities at the moment."

"I need to take some time for myself today. How about we reschedule for another day?"

assert yourself

Obstacles do not block the path, they are the path.

Zen proverb

If you become too passive or submissive, you will end up carrying a lot of pent-up frustrations. Learn to assert yourself and find solutions that won't leave you feeling wronged.

Some good ways of asserting yourself include getting your thoughts straight and knowing what you want to say before you start speaking. This will help you to work out what your priorities before you start the conversation.

If you struggle to assert yourself because you're lacking in confidence, just channel a really confident friend or colleague. What would they do or say in your situation? What kind of words or phrases do they use that help them to sound confident? If you know them well, you can even ask them for advice.

get enough sleep

Tired minds don't plan well. Sleep first, plan later.

Walter Reisch, film director and screenwriter

Go to bed earlier to ensure you get a full eight hours of sleep. When we're frazzled and grumpy life does not go smoothly! Studies have shown that even minor sleep disturbances can impact on our memory, concentration and mood.

If you struggle to get to sleep or stay asleep, do everything you can to make your room a cosy and calm environment. Go for dim lighting and make sure the temperature isn't too high or too low. If you've tried every trick in the book and you are still struggling with your sleep, book an appointment with your doctor.

try aromatherapy

Smell is a potent wizard that transports you across thousands
of miles and all the years you have lived.

*Helen Keller, author, disability rights advocate, political activist
and lecturer*

Sometimes called essential oil therapy, aromatherapy
works by using essential oils as an aid for better health
and wellbeing. It can help with improving your sleep,
reducing feeling of stress and anxiety and can also help
with treating minor headaches.

Add a few drops of relaxing essential oils to your bath,
or massage them into your feet for an instant soothing
effect. Popular essential oils include lavender, ylang
ylang and tea tree.

select a centring object

Find your centre and live in it.

Ralph Waldo Trine, philosopher and author

Choose an object such as a smooth pebble you can keep in your pocket, or a locket around your neck. Touch this object whenever you're feeling stressed or anxious to centre you and help calm your thoughts.

It doesn't matter what the object is; it doesn't have to hold any special meaning (though sometimes this can help), and it doesn't have to be something of great value. It just needs to be something distinct enough that, each time you touch it or play with it in your hand, it serves as an instant reminder to take a few deep breaths and to centre yourself.

learn to love your enemy

Those who tried to break you are expecting you to be in fight mode. Conquer them with your peace.

Dr Thema Davis, professor of psychology

Harbouring resentments toward perceived "enemies" is really going to kill your calm. Visualize your enemy as a much-loved friend or family member and you should find yourself feeling gentler thoughts toward them next time you are in their company.

Also try to think about why your so-called "enemies" act in the way they do. Have they been through hardships of their own that make them come across as hostile in certain situations? How have their experiences of life influenced the way they act around other people? Though sometimes difficult, it is essential to remember that every person has a story of their own, and, sometimes, just because they have a different view of what is "acceptable" doesn't mean they have to be an enemy.

plan to be calm

Patience is not the ability to wait. Patience is to be calm
no matter what happens, constantly take action to turn it
to positive growth opportunities, and have faith to believe
that it will all work out in the end while you are waiting.

Roy T. Bennett, writer and motivational speaker

While we can never know the exact outcome of any given
situation, we can make sensible predictions. If you have a
potentially stressful situation on the horizon, consider all
the possible outcomes and plan your reaction to each of
these ahead of time. It is much easier to stay calm if you've
already acted out doing just that in your head.

For example, if you have a job interview coming up and
you're worried about not being able to answer a question,
what could you use as a worst-case-scenario answer?
Though it may not be the perfect answer you would have
hoped to give, it can be calming to know that you have at
least something to work with in that situation.

slowly, slowly...

The day you stop racing, is the day you win the race.

Bob Marley, singer and songwriter

Living each moment rushing to get to the next is a surefire way to increase tension throughout the body and mind. You may feel as though you have no choice but to rush, but there is always an option to slow down. In fact, everything will improve if you do – your work, your health and your state of mind.

Sometimes, there may be instances where your racing around is in fact slowing you down. This is because when you are hurrying to get through several tasks you are in a constant state of stress and are unlikely to be thinking straight – your brain will be tired from working at a hundred miles an hour and you are more likely to miss the finer details which could result in mistakes.

The next time you feel yourself rushing through something, take a deep breath and try to go slower. More haste, less speed!

sing your heart out

The only thing better than singing is more singing.

Ella Fitzgerald, jazz singer

Singing has been proven to release feel-good hormones that reduce stress and anxiety. Consider joining a choir for the added benefit of human connectivity.

Studies have shown that choristers' heartbeats synchronize when they sing together, bringing about a communal calming effect and a sense of togetherness. Singing in a group has even been shown to help people deal with feelings of grief, and can also help to improve overall happiness and wellbeing.

take a hot bath

I love the magic of a hot bath, how time pauses and every grievance passes away.

Richelle E. Goodrich, writer

When we are stressed, our muscles naturally become more tense. For example, we tend to clench our stomach muscles or hold our shoulders up too high. Taking a hot bath can help to reduce these problems by helping us to relax our muscles. Not only is it soothing and relaxing, it can also help to improve blood circulation, and is therefore great as a form of natural pain relief.

As the heat relaxes your muscles and eases any aches and pains, then so your mind relaxes. For extra calm, add candles and a rose-scented bath oil.

lay your head on a pillow

A ruffled mind makes a restless pillow.

Charlotte Brontë, novelist

While your day may not allow time out for a nap, you can always take just a minute or two to reset. Lay your head on a pillow and visualize all your worries and stresses soaking into the pillow as if it were a sponge. After a couple of minutes, raise your head feeling calmer and rejuvenated.

When you're feeling stressed and anxious, it can also help to simply hug a pillow. Studies have shown that hugging something soft can help to improve your overall wellbeing by inducing a feeling of calm and safety, helping you to relax not only mentally, but physically too.

Pillows also come in all shapes and sizes – you can even get ones that you can wrap around yourself – so pick one that makes you feel extra cosy and calm, ready for whenever you need it.

smell the roses

Take time to smell the roses. Appreciating the little things in life really can make all the difference.

Andy Puddicombe, author and public speaker

The soothing scents of flowers can stimulate smell receptors in the nose that connect to the part of the brain that regulates emotions. So next time you're feeling overwhelmed by stress, take some time out to smell the roses. If you don't have any flowers to hand, you can instead light a floral-scented candle to fill your home with your favourite scent.

When it comes to soothing smells, it doesn't have to be just flowers. Think about all the scents that make you feel safe and calm or bring you some kind of joy. Perhaps it's the smell of freshly cut grass, your partner's clothing, bread in the oven or the pages of an old book. When you're having a bad day, see if you can seek out your favourite smells to help bring you a sense of peace and calm.

stretch

A heart at peace gives life to the body.

Book of Proverbs, the Bible

There are many health benefits – both mental and physical – that come with stretching your body regularly. Stretching is great for reducing tension in your body and improving your posture, especially if you've been sitting at your desk all day while at work. This reduction in physical tension will help to reduce mental stress, too, helping you to clear your head and improve focus.

You don't need lots of space to practise regular stretching – you can do it anywhere, even at your desk. Stretch your arms out above your head and gently twist your torso from side to side. And don't forget your neck and your shoulders, too.

If you spend a large part of your day at a desk, it is recommended that you take at least 5–10 minutes every hour to stretch your body and get your blood flowing again.

socialize

Sometimes just spending time with friends is the only therapy you need.

Unknown

Socializing is a great stress reliever. Spend time with groups of good friends and the interaction will help you to unwind effortlessly. Spending time with friends and family also helps give you a sense of purpose and belonging.

Though text messaging and video calls mean it's never been easier to keep in touch with your loved ones, you should also arrange to see people in person, as nothing can beat face-to-face interaction. If your friends and family live far away, find out if there are any local clubs or reading groups that might be of interest to you. These are a great way to ensure that you are meeting people regularly without the hassle of always having to arrange a time and place. Alongside joining a club, volunteering in your local community is also an excellent way of meeting new people.

listen to yourself

**Follow your instincts. That's where true wisdom
manifests itself.**

Oprah Winfrey, talk show host

If you find yourself losing your patience easily and you're
having more trouble than usual staying calm, it's time to
take a step back and ask yourself why.

Are you working too many long hours without a break?
Take a couple of days off to recharge your batteries. Not
taking enough time out for self-care? Schedule in more
time to do the things that relax you and bring you back to
your true self. Feeling tired and unfocused? Try to get more
sleep and to eat as healthily as possible.

The more you start to listen to what your body is telling
you, the quicker you will be able to recognize when
something isn't quite right.

turn the volume down

In silence there is eloquence. Stop weaving and see how the
pattern improves.

Rumi, poet

In a world where we have multiple personal devices
on which we can access endless amounts of information,
stream libraries of music and films, or find out what
our friends are doing – all with the click of a button –
it's all too easy to fill moments of stillness with "doing
something".

However, these moments of stillness and silence should
be treated as precious. Turn off the TV and radio, shut
down your computer, switch your phone to silent and let
your mind wander in the emptiness of the moment. Carve
out regular time for this quiet contemplation.

ditch the drama

Saying nothing sometimes says the most.

Emily Dickinson, Victorian author and poet

Anyone who generates drama in your life is having a negative impact. Perhaps you've got a friend who picks petty arguments with you out of nowhere or a friend who constantly jumps to conclusions when something goes wrong. These relationships are toxic and aren't worth your precious time and energy.

Engage instead in harmonious relationships with people who enhance your sense of wellbeing, who make you feel great about yourself whenever you spend time with them.

If you yourself are the kind of person who has tendencies to generate drama, ask yourself why. Do you need to practise accepting other people's differences? Do you need to work on more effective ways of communicating with your friends and family?

try transcendental
meditation

Nowhere can man find a quieter or more untroubled retreat
than in his own soul.

Marcus Aurelius, Roman emperor

This meditation technique involves sitting in silence for
20 minutes or more and repeating a mantra. It's wonderful
for quieting a chattering mind and achieving true stillness
in times of stress or anxiety.

1. Close your eyes and bring your mantra to mind.

2. As your mind wanders become aware that you are no
   longer hearing your mantra. This awareness alone will
   enable you to return effortlessly to it.

3. Toward the end of meditation bring your attention
   back to your body and the room you are in for a few
   minutes before opening your eyes.

be realistic

Patience is seeing each step as a journey rather than seeing a journey as a thousand steps.

Richelle E. Goodrich, writer

If you are finding yourself stressed and overwhelmed, are you being realistic about what you can achieve? Perhaps you feel like you are always busy and complaining of not having enough time in the day, when really you've just got too much on your to-do list. Or perhaps you're frustrated by not being able to complete certain tasks at work, even though you haven't received proper training or don't have the same level of experience as your colleagues.

Reset your goals so they are attainable and stop reaching for unrealistic standards that will leave you feeling like you're always running to catch up. Constantly feeling as though you are always trying to reach something, only to never quite make it, will only increase thoughts of failure and as though you aren't good enough. Be true to yourself, and set goals in line with your own unique set of skills.

dance

I crowded far too many tasks into Yesterday. Today is now demanding music, chocolate truffles, and sporadic dancing, as compensation.

Dr SunWolf, professor, author, social scientist and attorney

If you don't have the time or the inclination to attend regular dance classes, simply bust your moves on the kitchen (dance) floor. Dancing to your favourite tunes will release mood-boosting endorphins and ease any pent-up tension.

If you're somebody who finds the gym or going for a jog boring, dancing is a more exciting form of exercise and a good way to get your whole body moving. You don't need to be part of a club – just stick some music on wherever you've got some space and get moving. Dancing in your own home is also great if you're particularly self-conscious, as no one will be able to see you! Turn the music up and have some fun.

give up control

**Don't let your mind bully your body into believing it must
carry the burden of its worries.**

Terri Guillemets, writer

It's time to let go of any control-freak tendencies if you
want to achieve true inner harmony. Let go of those
situations and people you cannot control. In any situation
ask yourself, "What can I do about this?". If it can't be
changed, accept it and move on.

You may also find that you need to work harder at trusting
other people. For example, if you've organized a fun day
out for you and your friends, and you know you have a
tendency to dominate, do your best to take a back seat and
let others look after things.

stop procrastinating

Procrastination is the thief of time.

Edward Young, poet

Put effort into solving problems that are weighing heavy on your mind. More often than not, you'll know exactly what needs doing to resolve these niggles but spend too long procrastinating over them.

Think about why you tend to procrastinate. Is a fear of failure stopping you from starting a task? Do you not want to begin a certain project because you aren't quite sure where to start? These feelings are very common, but the best thing you can do is to just get going. When you delay starting something, you're only putting more pressure on yourself as you're giving yourself less and less time to complete it. By simply just starting a task, and breaking it down into smaller sections, you will feel less overwhelmed by it, and will be able to stop spending precious time overthinking things.

timeless challenge

And indeed, there will be time...

T.S. Eliot, author and poet

This may sound a little crazy at first, but it will teach you a lot about your needs and how to listen to what your body is telling you.

Cover all the clocks in your house (and also do your best to not look at the time on your phone), and see if you can go a whole day without knowing what time it is. Eat when you are hungry, take a break when you feel you need it, go for a walk if you feel your body start to become stiff and tense, sleep when you feel tired.

This can be a truly fascinating challenge. All too often we pigeonhole ourselves into doing certain things at certain times of the day. For or example, we may eat lunch between twelve and one o'clock, not because we are hungry but because we are told that this is lunchtime. But truly listening to your needs will allow you to connect with your body and mind in a way you may not ever have done before.

meditate on art

Art is an irreplaceable way of understanding and expressing the world.

Dana Gioia, poet, literary critic and essayist

Pick a piece of art such as a painting and set aside five minutes to meditate on it. How does it make you feel? What do you observe as you look further into the artwork? What details can you now see that you missed at first glance? What story arises in your mind as you view the art?

An art gallery is an excellent place to do this, not only because you'll have access to a huge amount of art, but because these spaces are usually fairly quiet, giving you the space and stillness to be able to truly reflect upon what you are seeing.

question your thoughts

Do not anticipate trouble or worry about what may never
happen. Keep in the sunlight.

Benjamin Franklin, founding father of the United States

Try to become aware of your thoughts and you will start
to notice when you fall into negative patterns of thinking
that disrupt your inner peace. For example, do you tend to
talk yourself out of certain things because you worry about
them being too difficult? Do you find yourself jumping to
conclusions in certain situations, before you know all the
facts? Do you tend to overthink and worry about the future
even though you have no way of knowing what's in store?

Whenever these kinds of thoughts pop into your mind,
acknowledge them, and then ask yourself why they've
come up. The more attuned you become to your mind's
natural rhythm, the more you'll be able to control your
thought processes, and the more you will be able to stop
these negative thoughts in their tracks, before they cause
any further damage.

practise acupressure

Touch the body, heal the mind, calm the spirit.

Unknown

Going for a massage is not always an option, but you can easily and quickly practise techniques such as acupressure on yourself.

Try pressing your thumb on the point where the inside of your wrist forms a crease with your hand for two minutes to release tension. This is a great exercise that you can do anywhere, whether you're at home or in the office.

If you're at home and you've got a little more space, you can also use an acupressure mat. These are plastic mats that have hundreds of points on them, which you can either walk across or lie on top of. These mats may be a little painful at first, but the more you practise using them the easier they will be to use. However, only use these mats for as long as is comfortable for you – you should never stay too long in any sharp pain.

cultivate routine

Slow down and everything you are chasing will come around
and catch you.

John de Paola, writer

Having a daily routine can really help to increase your
overall wellbeing by managing your stress levels, helping
you to eat more healthily and regularly, and ensuring that
you get a good amount of sleep each night.

Having a routine will also eliminate the chance of
becoming overworked and burned out. For example, if
you promise yourself to always stop and eat dinner at
seven o'clock, you'll be less tempted to work late or take
on responsibilities that take up your time in the evening.
If you promise yourself you're always going to be asleep
before midnight, you'll be less likely to spend time binging
TV shows late into the night, and will be more likely to get
a good night's sleep.

ask for help

The only mistake you can make is not asking for help.

Dr Sandeep Jauhar, cardiologist and author

You don't always have to do everything by yourself. Use your support system of friends or family when you're in need. Trying to take on the world and do everything solo will lead to a state of constant stress and worry, and isn't a realistic way to live your life.

You may worry that, when you ask your friends and family for help, you are becoming a burden to them, but this is simply not the case. Those who truly love and care for you will always be there to give you a hand when the going gets tough. Those who are not there to help are not your true friends.

close your eyes

To see your inner self, close your eyes and feel.

Dr Debasish Mridha, philosopher and author

This is such a simple technique to regain inner calm and composure – block out the world for a few seconds just by lowering your eyelids.

Studies have shown that closing your eyes for a few short moments can almost be effective as sleep. Though, of course, simply closing your eyes will not kick-start the cycles of sleep, it will encourage your body to relax your muscles, helping to ease any tension in your body. Closing your eyes and blocking out the world will also give your brain a much-needed rest. You'll find that even just ten minutes of doing so will leave you feeling more alert, energized and with a clearer, calmer mind.

prioritize peace

How beautiful it is to do nothing, and then to rest afterwards.

Spanish proverb

Will you look back on your life and wish you had rushed about more in a frazzled manner, or will you celebrate the moments of calm and connectedness; relationships and experiences that you fully embraced and enjoyed in the moment?

Peace, calm and happiness should always be the ultimate goals in our lives. If you are putting things like work and chores ahead of the things that make you happy, you need to take a step back and re-evaluate your life. What changes can you make to ensure that your happiness is revolving around things like work, rather than the other way around?

Life is far too short to be worrying about the things that, ultimately, do not matter. Prioritize peace, and live your life to the full.